The School Track Meet

Understand Place Value

Alex Zander

NEW YORK

Published in 2014 by The Rosen Publishing Group, Inc.
29 East 21st Street, New York, NY 10010

Book Design: Jon D'Rozario

Photo Credits: Cover Denis Kuvaev/Shutterstock.com; p. 5 (girl) bikeriderlondon/Shutterstock.com; p. 7 archideaphoto/Shutterstock.com; p. 9 (road) victoria9/Shutterstock.com; p. 9 (vehicles) PILart/Shutterstock.com; p. 11 (track) Matthew Cole/Shutterstock.com; p. 11 (jerseys) Sham619/Shutterstock.com; p. 13 (track) sunsetman/Shutterstock.com; p. 13 (hurdles) Tsurukame Design/Shutterstock.com; pp. 15, 17 (track) vichie81/Shutterstock.com; pp. 15, 17 (time clock) Antun Hirsman/Shutterstock.com; p. 19 (sand) Vitaly Korovin/Shutterstock.com; p. 19 (footprints) LongQuattro/Shutterstock.com; p. 21 (woodgrain) aliisik/Shutterstock.com; p. 21 (ribbon) SkillUp/Shutterstock.com; p. 21 (medal) Natykach Nataliia/Shutterstock.com; p. 22 Karkas/Shutterstock.com.

Library of Congress Cataloging-in-Publication Data

Zander, Alex.
School track meet: understand place value / by Alex Zander.
  p. cm. — (Core math skills: number and operations in base ten)
Includes index.
ISBN 978-1-477-2223-7 (library binding)
ISBN 978-1-4777-2040-0 (pbk.)
ISBN 978-1-4777-2041-7 (6-pack)
1. Arithmetic—Juvenile literature. 2. Mathematical notation—Juvenile literature. 3. Track and field—Juvenile literature. I. Title.
QA115.Z36 2014
510—dc23

Manufactured in the United States of America

CPSIA Compliance Information: Batch #CS13RC: For further information contact Rosen Publishing, New York, New York at 1-800-237-9932.

Word Count: 365

Contents

Place Value Is Fun!

Mia is learning about place value in math class.

Mia's teacher says that in a two-digit number,

the number on the left stands for tens.

The number on the right stands for ones.

1 tens 2 ones

You can use the tens and ones places to learn about numbers. They tell you which number's bigger, which one's smaller, or if the numbers are **equal**. Mia's going to practice this at the track meet after school!

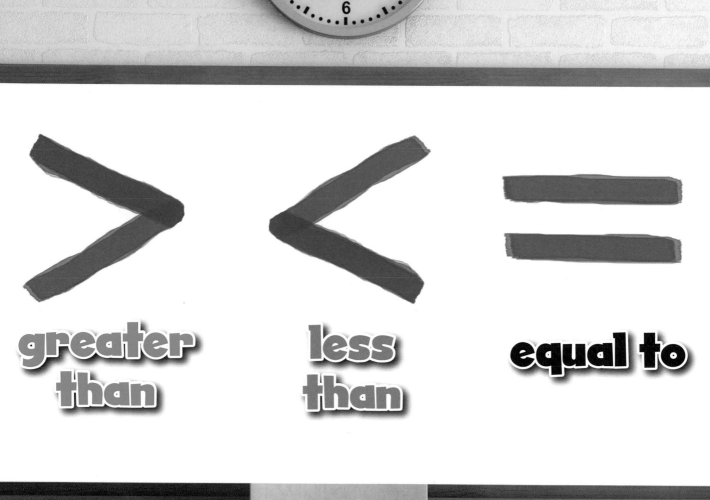

greater than **less than** **equal to**

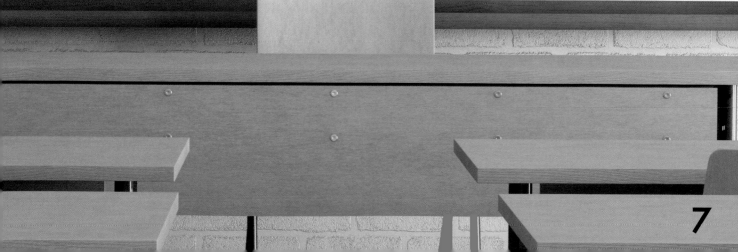

Going to the Meet

On the way to the meet, Mia sees 14 cars and 11 trucks. Both numbers have 1 ten. Mia counts the ones. The cars have 4 ones. The trucks have 1 one. There are more cars than trucks.

14

11

14 > 11

tens ones   tens ones

9

On the Team

There are 10 kids on Mia's track team. There are 10 kids on the other track team. They both have 1 ten and 0 ones. There are an equal number of kids on each team.

red team

blue team

10 kids

10 kids

10 = 10

tens ones   tens ones

11

At the Meet

One **event** at the track meet is the **hurdles**. There are 20 tall hurdles and 15 short hurdles. The tall hurdles have 2 tens. The short hurdles only have 1 ten. Mia knows there are more tall hurdles than short hurdles.

20

15

20 > 15

tens   ones   tens   ones

Soon, the races begin. Mia's friend Kaylee runs 1 lap in 35 seconds. Mia's friend Ryan runs 1 lap in 40 seconds. Mia knows that 3 tens is less than 4 tens. Ryan runs slower than Kaylee.

Kaylee

Ryan

35

40

35 < 40

tens   ones   tens   ones

15

It's Mia's turn to run! She runs 2 laps in 55 seconds. Her friend Emma also runs 2 laps in 55 seconds. Both times have 5 tens and 5 ones. Their times are equal.

Mia

Emma

55 = 55

tens ones   tens ones

17

The long jump is the next event. Mia jumps 67 inches. Her friend Tara jumps 61 inches. Mia counts the ones to see which jump was longer. Her score has 7 ones, while Tara's has 1. Mia's jump was longer than Tara's.

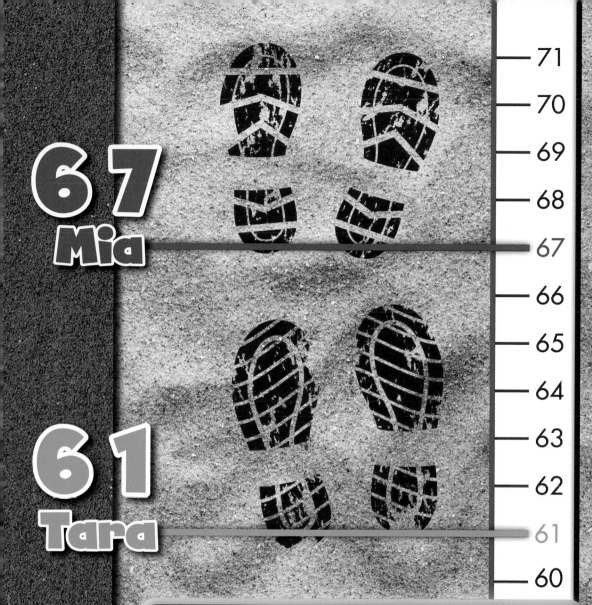

67 Mia

61 Tara

71
70
69
68
67
66
65
64
63
62
61
60

67 > 61
tens ones   tens ones

19

Time for Prizes!

When the meet is over, people get **medals** and **ribbons**. There are 13 medals. There are 20 ribbons. The medals have 1 ten, while the ribbons have 2 tens. The number of medals is less than the number of ribbons.

13   20

13 < 20

tens ones   tens ones

21

Everyone had a lot of fun at the track meet! It was fun to exercise. It was also fun to use place value to count things at the meet.

Glossary

equal (EE-kwuhl) The same.

event (ih-VEHNT) Something that happens.

hurdle (HUHR-duhl) An object with two legs and one bar that you jump over.

medal (MEH-duhl) A piece of metal people get when they win something.

ribbon (RIH-buhn) A piece of cloth people get when they win something.

Index